AF416579

THE FIVE KEYS TO PROSPERITY

Love Faith Truth Beauty Goodness

Edited for Young Adults Ages 30 — 45 (Younger or Older)

Wallace W. Frazier

Scriptor House LLC

17434 Bellflower Blvd Ste 200-188 Bellflower, CA 90706

www.scriptorhouse.com

Phone: +1209-554-8271

© 2026 Wallace W. Frazier. All rights reserved.

No part of this book may be reproduced, stored in a retrieval system, or transmitted by any means without the written permission of the author.

Published by Scriptor House LLC

Paperback: 979-8-88692-698-9
eBook: 979-8-88692-699-6

Because of the dynamic nature of the Internet, any web addresses or links contained in this book may have changed since publication and may no longer be valid. The opinions expressed in this manuscript are solely the opinions of the author and do not represent the opinions or thoughts of the publisher and the publisher hereby disclaims any

TABLE OF CONTENTS

PROLOGUE
LIFE'S SEASONS

Life unfolds in seasons, whether we recognize them or not. There are seasons of growth and expansion, seasons of waiting and uncertainty, seasons of pruning, and seasons of quiet restoration. Prosperity does not appear uniformly across time. It reveals itself progressively, as life aligns more deeply with its intended order.

Many people reach adulthood with expectations shaped by effort. Work hard, do what is right, remain faithful, and stability should follow. Yet somewhere between responsibility and reality, those expectations begin to fracture. Effort no longer guarantees outcome. Faith feels tested not by crisis, but by endurance. The weight of providing, deciding, and sustaining begins to press inward.

This is not failure.

It is transition.

Prosperity does not disappear in these seasons—it changes form. It becomes less about accumulation and more about peace. Less about control and more about alignment. Less about getting ahead and more about living well.

The Five Keys are not methods for escaping life's seasons. They are principles for moving through them wisely—without fear, without exhaustion, and without losing the soul in the process.

Your Notes:

Nurturing Fathers
Part I — Love
Perception, Identity, and the Fatherhood of God

Chapter One

Perceptions of God the Father and His Kingdom

What you believe about God quietly determines how you live.

Before money becomes an issue, perception of God is the issue. Before effort, planning, or discipline ever enter the picture, the image a person carries of God shapes how they approach life itself. A distorted image of God produces distorted expectations of provision, worth, and safety.

God is love—not merely loving, but love itself. This is not poetic language. It is foundational truth. When love is misunderstood, fear fills the gap. When fear governs perception, trust becomes fragile. And when trust erodes, prosperity feels uncertain and unsafe.

Many people struggle not because they lack faith, but because they have unknowingly adopted a conditional view of God. If God is perceived as distant, punitive, or withholding, life becomes transactional. They feel like worth must be proven. Blessing must be earned. Rest must be justified.

Jesus did not reveal God this way.

He consistently spoke of God as Father—present, generous, patient, and relational. This was not sentimental language. It was corrective language. He was restoring a damaged perception that had burdened people for generations.

To misunderstand God is to misunderstand the Kingdom. And the Kingdom of God does not begin somewhere else—it begins within.

The Urantia Book — Paper 2: "God and His Relation to the Universe"

God is fundamentally and eternally a loving Father. Love is the dominant and governing attribute of God's character, and the primary way humans experience divine reality is through trust in that love.

God's Love as the Foundation of Prosperity

Prosperity does not begin with effort.
It begins with worth.

When love is secure, fear loosens its grip. When identity is anchored, provision no longer feels threatening. People who know they are loved do not live anxiously. They plan wisely, work faithfully, and rest without guilt.

Many believers carry the belief that love must be earned—through obedience, sacrifice, or suffering. This belief quietly undermines faith. When love is conditional, peace is unstable. When peace is unstable, prosperity becomes something to chase rather than something to receive.

God's love is not a response to human performance. It is the starting point. Jesus never taught that people must become worthy before receiving. He taught that receiving transforms the heart, which then aligns your life with God's Will and purpose for your life.

Love precedes change.
It does not wait for it.

Prosperity built on love is sustainable. Prosperity built on fear collapses under pressure.

Your Notes:

The Kingdom Within You

Jesus taught that the Kingdom of God is within you. This statement reorients everything. The Kingdom is not enforced from the outside. It unfolds from alignment within.

The Kingdom operates through principles, not favoritism. Growth is progressive. Timing is purposeful. Provision flows through order rather than force.

This is why frantic striving produces diminishing returns. Anxiety cannot accelerate divine order. Control cannot replace trust. The Kingdom does not respond to pressure—it responds to harmony.

To live in the Kingdom is not to withdraw from responsibility. It is to engage life from a different center and perspective—one rooted in belonging rather than survival.

Your Notes:

Identity, Worth, and Receiving Without Guilt

One of the greatest obstacles to prosperity is not lack. It is guilt.

Many people feel unworthy of rest, joy, or provision unless they have suffered sufficiently. This belief does not originate in God. It originates in fear and distorted teaching. This is what Christ Jesus meant when he said, ***"Verily I say unto you, Except you be converted, and become as little children, you shall not enter into the kingdom of heaven."***

— Matthew 18:3

A child does not earn love.
They receive it.

Receiving without guilt is not entitlement. It is trust. And trust is the soil in which prosperity grows naturally.

When identity is rooted in divine love, effort becomes balanced. Overwork loses its grip. Fear of loss diminishes. Life begins to breathe again.

Love restores identity.
Identity restores peace.
Peace creates space for prosperity to unfold.

Your Notes:

Closing Reflection — LOVE

Love is not an abstract virtue. It is the foundation of alignment with God the Father. Before faith can stabilize, before truth can liberate, before beauty can restore meaning, and before goodness can guide action, love must be clarified.

You do not receive more by striving harder.
You receive more by trusting deeper.
Your entrance into the Kingdom begins here.

Your Notes:

Part II — Faith
Chapter Two

Trusting God When Outcomes Are Uncertain

How this picture portrays Faith

- A single adult (30s–40s) **mid-step**
- Ground ahead is **partially obscured**
- Light is present, but **destination is not visible**
- Body posture is steady, not rushed

Theological meaning

This image embodies **biblical faith as it is portrayed in the bible.**

"We walk by faith, not by sight." — 2 Corinthians 5:7

Faith here is:
- Action without guarantees
- Obedience before clarity
- Trust expressed through movement

The FAITH content emphasizes:
- Responsibility without certainty
- Provision that unfolds progressively
- Trust that acts without control

This image visually says:

"I don't see everything — but I'm moving anyway."

Your Notes:

Faith as Trust, Not Certainty

Faith as Steadiness Under Pressure

There is **no urgency or motion** in the image.

- No running
- No grasping
- No pleading posture

They are standing still — choosing to remain present in uncertainty.

This mirrors Christ's instruction:

"Take no thought for tomorrow..." (Matthew 6:34)

Faith here is **restful steadiness**, not forced optimism.

Your Notes:

Faith as Forward Orientation

He is not looking back.

- No regret posture
- No collapse
- No nostalgia

Faith, biblically, is always **forward-facing**:

"Forgetting those things which are behind…" (Philippians 3:13)

The image quietly communicates *orientation* — a key faith principle.

Your Notes:

PART III — TRUTH
CHAPTER THREE

Correction, Freedom, and the End of Exhaustion

How These Images Portrays False Agreement and Truth

TRUTH — A Tale of Two Postures

Before: Living Under False Agreements—The woman in left image

She is still doing the work.
But the work is doing her.

Her body is bent forward, shoulders drawn inward, mind racing ahead of the moment she is in. The desk is cluttered not only with papers, but with expectation — the unspoken belief that if she stops, something will collapse.

This is not laziness.
This is responsibility distorted by fear.

Here, effort is driven by false agreements:

- *If I slow down, I will fail.*
- *If I rest, I am being irresponsible.*
- *If I carry less, I am letting someone down.*

Nothing in the scene is immoral or wrong
And yet everything feels heavy.

This is what happens when truth is obscured — when devotion quietly turns into overextension, and faith is replaced by control.

After: Truth Restored, Burden Released—The woman in right image

Nothing external has changed.

The desk is still there.
The work remains.
Responsibilities have not vanished.
But something essential has shifted.

Her posture opens. Her hands release. Her breath deepens. She leans back not in avoidance, but in clarity. The urgency that once ruled her has lost its authority.

Your Notes:

This is not escape.
This is correction.

Truth has intervened — not by removing responsibility, but by removing what was never required. The false agreement has been broken:

- *I am faithful even when I rest.*
- *I am responsible without being consumed.*
- *God is present even when I release control.*

Truth restores right order.

And when right order returns, the soul and body respond together.

The Meaning of the Contrast

Burnout was never the price of faith.
Exhaustion was never the measure of devotion.

The difference between these two moments is not effort — it is **truth received**.

"You shall know the truth, and the truth shall make you free."

Freedom does not mean doing less.
It means carrying only what is yours to carry.

The Image portrays Truth as Release, Not Escape

The woman is still **at her desk**.
Work is present. Responsibility is not abandoned.

- Laptop open
- Papers still on the table
- The environment is real, not idealized

This matters because **truth does not remove responsibility** — it removes **false burden**.

Truth does not say, "Stop working."
Truth says, "Stop carrying what is not yours."

The image shows engagement with life **without internal strain**.

These images shows the **physical result of corrected belief contrasted to false agreements**.

When false agreements are released, the body responds first.

Truth restores **right order** internally before anything changes externally.

Truth Removes Compulsion, Not Effort

Notice what she is *not* doing:

- Not rushing
- Not grasping
- Not scanning papers anxiously
- Not checking the screen compulsively

Truth does not remove effort — it removes **compulsion**.

This aligns precisely with Jesus' correction:

Said Jesus, "Martha, Martha, You are fretting and worrying about so many things: But there is only one thing that is needful…Mary has chosen the right thing, and it won't be taken away from her. (Luke 10:41–42)

The image on the right shows effort without turmoil.

Truth as Inner Alignment

The light entering the room is natural, not dramatic.

- No beams
- No spectacle
- No supernatural effects

This is important.

Truth is not a shock — it is an adjustment.

False beliefs collapse quietly when truth is received.

The calm light signals **clarity**, not dramatic revelation.

Truth Reveals That Burnout Was Not Required

The most important message the image sends is subtle:

"I did not need to suffer this much to be faithful."

That realization is **truth**.

Burnout often persists because people believe it is:

- Necessary
- Noble
- Spiritually expected

Truth dissolves that belief — and the body relaxes when it does.

Why This Image Is TRUTH (Not BEAUTY or FAITH)

- **Not FAITH** → no forward movement, no step into unknown
- **Not BEAUTY** → joy is present, but meaning is not the focus

- **Not LOVE** → care is implicit, not relationally depicted

This image shows:

Correction that brings freedom

That is TRUTH.

Your Notes:

CHAPTER THREE—TRUTH

When Alignment Replaces Overwork

Truth does not burden the soul.
It relieves it.

Many people are exhausted not because they lack discipline, faith, or commitment, but because they are living under **false agreements** they never consciously chose. These agreements quietly shape how they work, how they rest, and how they measure their worth.

By the time many adults reach their thirties and forties, exhaustion is no longer physical. It is internal. It is the fatigue of carrying beliefs that were never meant to be carried.

Truth does not accuse these beliefs.
It exposes them — and exposure is liberation.

Your Notes:

False Agreements and the Cost of Overwork

A false agreement is a belief that feels responsible but is not true.

Common false agreements include:

- *My value depends on my productivity.*
- *If I stop, everything will fall apart.*
- *Rest must be earned.*
- *God expects constant effort.*

These beliefs often masquerade as virtue. They sound mature. They feel necessary, and they even feel spiritual or religious. Yet over time, they quietly produce burnout, anxiety, and resentment.

Jesus never taught that worth was earned through exhaustion.

Instead, He consistently corrected the belief that God measures people by output rather than by relationship.

Said Jesus, "Come unto me, all you that labor and are heavy laden, and I will give you rest." — Gospel of Matthew 11:28

This invitation is not poetic sentiment. It is a **truth correction**. It directly challenges the belief that constant labor is spiritually required.

Your Notes:

Truth Restores Right Order

Truth is not merely accurate information.
Truth restores order.

Order between:

- Effort and trust
- Responsibility and surrender
- Action and rest

When order is lost, effort expands endlessly. When order is restored, effort becomes effective again.

Scripture affirms this restoration of order:

"Except the Lord build the house, they labor in vain that build it."
— Book of Psalms 127:1

This verse does not condemn labor.
It condemns labor divorced from alignment with God's Will and His purpose for your life.

Truth does not reduce effort.
It removes *vain* effort.

Your Notes:

Burnout Is Not Failure — It Is a Signal

Burnout is often misinterpreted as weakness or lack of faith. In reality, burnout is frequently a **signal of misalignment**, not moral failure.

People burn out when they:

- Carry responsibility meant to be shared with God
- Confuse faithfulness with overextension
- Substitute effort for trust

Truth does not shame burnout.
It diagnoses it.

And diagnosis is the beginning of healing.

Your Notes:

Jesus and the Correction of Religious Pressure

Jesus' strongest words were often reserved not for sinners, but for conditioning systems that burdened people while claiming divine authority.

Said Jesus, "They bind heavy burdens and grievous to be borne, and lay them on men's shoulders; but they themselves will not move them with one of their fingers." — Gospel of Matthew 23:4

Truth confronts religious pressure that masquerades as obedience.

Jesus did not oppose discipline.
He opposed **burdens that God never imposed**.

Your Notes:

TRUTH — Urantia Book and Scripture References

The Urantia Book offers language that complements — not replaces — this biblical correction, especially regarding burnout and false responsibility.

The Urantia Book, Paper 100 — "Religion in Human Experience"

(Paraphrased for accessibility)

Spiritual exhaustion often arises when individuals attempt to carry religious obligations without the inner assurance of divine partnership. True faith lightens responsibility rather than increasing it.

The Urantia Book, Paper 102 — "The Foundations of Religious Faith"

(Paraphrased)

Truth is not meant to enslave human effort but to free them. When religious belief produces anxiety and overstrain, it signals misunderstanding rather than devotion.

Why these references reinforces the concept of Truth.

- They reinforce Jesus' correction of burdens
- They frame burnout as misunderstanding, not sin
- They support *alignment over overexertion*

- They do **not** introduce new doctrine or chronology

They echo — rather than redefine Scripture.

Your Notes:

Truth Frees the Soul to Rest Without Fear of Self condemnation

Truth does not demand perfection.
It invites correction.

When false agreements are released:

- Rest becomes restorative instead of threatening
- Work becomes purposeful instead of compulsive
- Faith becomes sustainable instead of fragile

This is why Jesus could say:

"If you abide in My Words, then are you My disciple and you shall know the truth and the truth shall make you free." — Gospel of John 8:32

Freedom is not the absence of responsibility.
It is the presence of right order.

Closing Reflection — TRUTH

Truth is not harsh.
It is merciful.

It does not accuse effort.
It removes what was never required.

When truth is received, the soul exhales.
And in that exhale, alignment returns.

One-Sentence Summary

Truth restores right order — and when false burdens are released, the soul and body exhale together.

Part IV — Beauty
Chapter Four

Restoring Meaning, Joy, And The Experience Of Life

BEAUTY — When Life Feels Alive Again

There is a kind of poverty that has nothing to do with money.

It is the poverty of meaning.

Many people do not suffer because they lack provision, but because life has become mechanical. Days are filled with responsibility, efficiency, and decision-making — all necessary, all demanding — yet something essential quietly disappears.

Joy fades gradually.
Wonder dulls imperceptibly.
Life continues, but it feels thin.

This is not rebellion.
It is fatigue of the soul.

Beauty is not a luxury.
It is nourishment.

Your Notes:

Beauty Restores What Truth Exposes

Truth corrects false beliefs.
But correction alone is not enough.

Once false burdens are released, the soul is left open — and what fills that space matters. Without beauty, life becomes technically correct but emotionally barren.

Beauty restores meaning where duty once dominated.

Jesus did not teach truth alone. He taught with stories, images, rhythm, and nature. He pointed to lilies, birds, fields, children. He restored perception before demanding obedience.

Beauty prepares the heart to receive truth **without resistance**.

Your Notes:

The Loss of Beauty in Adult Life

Many adults abandon beauty unintentionally.

Not because they reject joy — but because survival crowds it out.

Beauty feels impractical when:

- Time is scarce
- Responsibility is constant
- Outcomes feel urgent

Yet when beauty disappears, motivation eventually collapses. Life becomes functional but joyless. Prosperity without beauty feels hollow.

Beauty is not indulgence.
It is integration.

Your Notes:

Beauty as Presence, Not Escape

Beauty does not require travel, leisure, or wealth.

It requires **attention**.

The ability to pause without guilt.
To notice without rushing.
To receive without justifying.

When beauty returns:

- Time softens
- Anxiety loosens
- Meaning resurfaces

This is why beauty feels restorative — not because it changes circumstances, but because it **changes how life is experienced**.

Your Notes:

Scripture and Urantia Book references

Scripture consistently affirms beauty as part of divine order:

"He hath made everything beautiful in his time."
— **Ecclesiastes 3:11**

Beauty is not accidental.
It is intentional.

And Jesus affirmed beauty even in simplicity:

"Consider the lilies of the field, how they grow…"
— **Gospel of Matthew 6:28**

This is not an argument against work.
It is an argument against *joyless* living.

BEAUTY — Urantia Book References (Carefully Framed)

The Urantia Book complements this understanding of beauty without altering doctrine.

The Urantia Book, Paper 44 — "The Celestial Artisans"

(Paraphrased, not quoted)

Beauty is a spiritual reality that uplifts the mind and restores harmony between thought, feeling, and purpose.

The Urantia Book, Paper 56 — "Universal Unity"

(Paraphrased)

Beauty functions as a bridge between truth and goodness, making spiritual reality experiential rather than merely conceptual.

Closing Reflection — BEAUTY

What Beauty is not and what it does

- Beauty is not emotionalism
- Beauty restores *experience*
- Beauty supports truth and prepares for goodness

Beauty does not demand effort.
It invites awareness.

When beauty is restored, life feels worth living again — not because it became easier, but because it became meaningful.

Prosperity without beauty is survival.
Beauty restores the joy of being alive.

Your Notes:

PART V — GOODNESS

This picture represents Goodness as Aligned Action (Not Sacrifice)

No one is suffering.

No one is posturing.

No one is being highlighted as a "hero."

They are simply **doing what is right**, together, within their capacity.

This visually reinforces the core GOODNESS principle:

Goodness flows naturally when life is ordered.

Goodness Without Guilt or Martyrdom

Notice what is *absent*:

- No exhaustion
- No urgency
- No moral pressure
- No emotional manipulation

This matters, because the book "The Five Keys To Prosperity" explicitly rejects:

- Self-erasure as virtue
- Burnout as holiness
- Sacrifice as proof of goodness

Instead, the image shows **sustainable service**.

Community, Not Individual Moral Performance

Goodness in Scripture is rarely solitary.

This image shows:

- Shared responsibility
- Cooperation
- Mutual dignity

It visually supports:

"As we have opportunity, let us do good unto all men." (Galatians 6:10)

Opportunity — not compulsion.

The Picture Portrays Diversity Without Tokenism

- Multiple ethnicities
- Similar age range (30 or younger–45 or older)
- No single focal subject

This reinforces a quiet but powerful truth:

Goodness belongs to the human family.

No group owns it.

No culture monopolizes it.

This image shows:

Action after alignment

That is GOODNESS.

One-Sentence Caption

Goodness is alignment made visible—love lived wisely, faith applied patiently, truth enacted gently.

Your Notes:

Chapter Five

Aligned Action, Stewardship, and Living What Is True

Goodness in Action — When Right Living Becomes Natural

Goodness is not something you force.
It is something that **flows**.

Many people sincerely want to live good lives. They want to help others, do what is right, and contribute meaningfully. Yet over time, goodness can become heavy.

Giving becomes stressful.
Service becomes draining.
Responsibility becomes endless.

This is not because goodness demands too much — it is because goodness has been separated from **alignment**.

True goodness does not begin with obligation.
It begins with order.

Your Notes:

Prosperity, Ethics, and Responsibility

Prosperity raises ethical questions.

Is it right to want more?
Is provision selfish?
Does abundance compromise faith?

These questions often trouble thoughtful believers — especially those carrying responsibility for families, employees, or communities.

Goodness reframes the conversation.

Prosperity is not moral failure when it is governed by wisdom, generosity, and restraint. Neither poverty nor wealth is inherently virtuous. What matters is **stewardship**.

Goodness asks:

- How is provision used?
- Who is served by it?
- Does it restore life or deplete it?

Your Notes:

Giving, Service, and Sustainable Goodness

Giving is meant to be life-giving — not self-erasing.

Many people confuse generosity with depletion. They give beyond capacity, neglect personal responsibility, and then quietly resent the very goodness they sought to embody.

This is not divine generosity.
It is misdirected responsibility.

Goodness requires discernment.

Wise giving:

- Honors capacity
- Preserves dignity
- Strengthens the giver and the receiver

Sustainable goodness serves without destroying the source.

Your Notes:

GOODNESS — (Supporting Section)

Stewardship Versus Sacrifice

Sacrifice is often misunderstood.

Some were taught that God demands loss to prove devotion. Yet throughout Scripture, God consistently affirms life, growth, and fruitfulness.

Stewardship is not loss — it is **care**.

Stewardship asks:

- What has been entrusted to me?
- How do I manage it wisely?
- How does it serve life beyond myself?

Goodness guided by stewardship creates lasting impact without regret.

Your Notes:

Part V — Goodness (Closing Reflection)

Goodness is alignment expressed through action.

It is love lived wisely.

Faith applied patiently.

Truth enacted gently.

Beauty shared generously.

When goodness flows from alignment, action no longer drains the soul. Life becomes coherent again.

This is the final key.

Your Notes:

ABUNDANCE AND WEALTH

Abundance comes in many forms. Among the most rewarding is the Abundance of shared relationships with family, friends and loved ones.

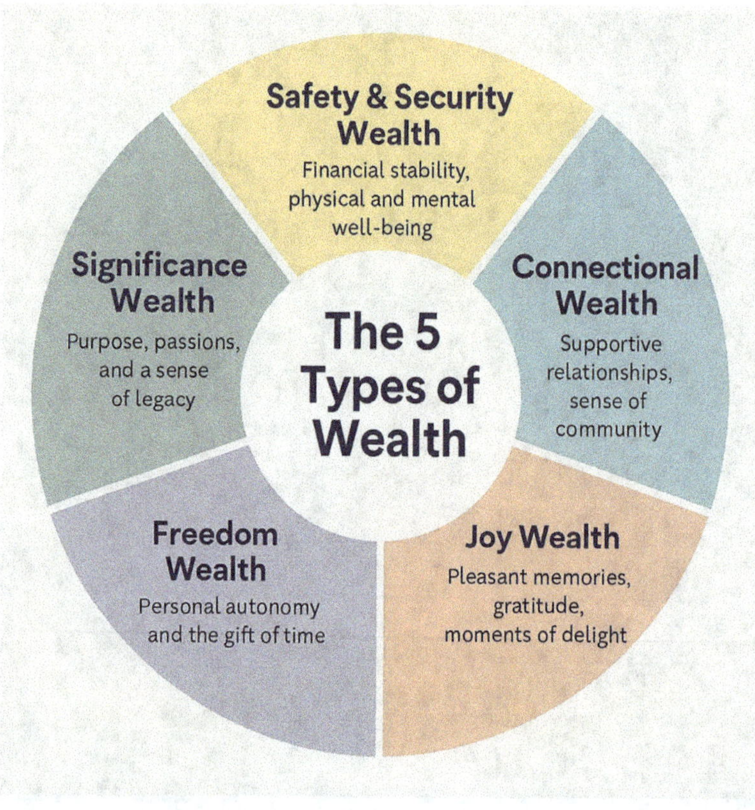

When the Five Keys are applied throughout life, Abundance and Wealth in their many forms are the inevitable result, and it flows naturally. Little or no effort is required to sustain True Abundance.

EPILOGUE
ABUNDANCE

Abundance is not something you chase.

It is what remains when life is brought into alignment with God's purpose for your life..

Many people spend years striving for more—more security, more freedom, more margin—believing abundance lies somewhere ahead. Yet abundance is not found by accelerating effort. It is revealed when resistance fades.

When love clarifies who God is, fear loosens its grip. When faith steadies the heart, uncertainty loses power. When truth corrects false agreements, effort becomes sustainable. When beauty restores meaning, life becomes livable again. When goodness flows naturally, action no longer drains the soul.

Abundance is not excess. It is wholeness.

Abundance as Peace, Not Pressure

True abundance feels calm. It is the quiet confidence that provision is sufficient, the relief of no longer measuring worth by productivity, and the ability to give without fear and to receive without guilt.

For many adults in mid-life, abundance does not mean having everything—it means finally having enough.

Enough clarity. Enough trust. Enough rest.

Enough to live well.

Abundance and Time

Abundance unfolds in seasons. Just as growth in nature follows rhythm and order, prosperity follows alignment with God's Will and purpose for your life rather than by force. Life expands when it is allowed to mature, not rushed toward completion.

Some spiritual traditions describe the universe itself as governed by progressive growth—where nothing is wasted, nothing is hurried, and nothing is withheld arbitrarily. Whether one interprets this theologically, spiritually, or practically, the message is consistent: life works best when lived in harmony with its design.

You Were Never Meant to Carry It Alone

Perhaps the greatest illusion of scarcity is the belief that everything depends on you.

It does not.

You were created to participate—not to perform alone, not to control outcomes, not to secure your future by strain.

Abundance begins when you release what was never yours to carry and accept partnership with the One, God the First Source and Center who sustains all things.

The Door Is Already Open

The Five Keys were never meant to unlock something distant. They unlock what has always been near.

Abundance is not waiting for you to become perfect. It is waiting for you to become aligned.

And alignment begins—not with striving—but with trust.

Final Note to the Reader

You do not need to master these principles. You only need to live them gently, faithfully, and honestly. Abundance will follow.

Your Notes:

Summary of the Book
The Five Keys To Prosperity"

The book, " **The Five Keys To Prosperity** " by Wallace W. Frazier, explores the concept of faith as a practical tool for spiritual, material, and personal growth including good health and wellbeing, especially during challenging times. It emphasizes the importance of understanding and applying spiritual faith to manifest desired outcomes and live a fulfilling life. The author discusses various aspects of faith, including its precepts, application, and the process of manifestation.

Key points include:

1. **Faith as a Tool**: Faith is described as more than belief; it is a practical mechanism to access spiritual and material prosperity. It involves hope, belief, trust, and action.

2. **Spiritual Growth**: The book encourages readers to seek truth, beauty, and goodness, and to live a Spirit-led life by aligning their will with God's will.

3. **Seasons of Life**: Life is seen as a series of seasons—cultivating, sowing, growing, harvesting, and feasting—each with its own lessons and opportunities for growth and prosperity.

4. **Overcoming Obstacles**: The book identifies destroyers of faith, such as doubt, fear, guilt, and negative attitudes, and

emphasizes the importance of overcoming these barriers to fully apply faith.

5. **Personal Relationship with God**: It stresses the significance of acknowledging God as the Universal Father and developing a personal relationship with Him through prayer, meditation, and service to others.

6. **True Religion vs. Institutional Religion**: The author contrasts institutionalized religion, which often imposes rituals and traditions, with the true religion of Christ Jesus, which focuses on seeking and doing God's will.

7. **Spiritual Reality**: The book introduces the concept of spiritual beings, ministering spirits, and celestial personalities that assist humans in their journey toward spiritual perfection.

8. **Faith Application Process**: Practical steps for applying faith include asking, seeking, knocking, recognizing life's seasons, and performing necessary actions to manifest the objects of faith.

The book also critiques traditional religious practices, challenges misconceptions about biblical scripture, and encourages readers to seek deeper spiritual truths beyond institutional religion. It draws heavily on biblical references and the Urantia Book to support its teachings. Ultimately, it aims to inspire readers to live by faith, embrace their identity as children of God, and achieve spiritual and material prosperity through the application of faith.

Your Notes:

What is the role of the Holy Spirit in Faith?

According to the book, the **Holy Spirit plays a vital role in faith** by providing guidance, comfort, and enlightenment to individuals as they seek to apply their faith and grow spiritually. The Holy Spirit helps believers discern truth, overcome obstacles like doubt and fear, and align their actions with God's will. Here are the key roles of the Holy Spirit in faith:

1. **Guidance and Direction**: The Holy Spirit leads individuals in understanding God's will and reveals the actions they need to take to manifest their faith objects. It helps believers recognize opportunities and doors that open in their lives.

2. **Comfort and Assurance**: The Holy Spirit provides comfort during trials, tribulations, and moments of doubt, offering reassurance that all things work together for good for those who love God.

3. **Discernment of Truth**: The Holy Spirit enhances the ability to recognize and confirm spiritual truths, coordinating with the Spirit of Truth to purge errors and inspire individuals to seek and accept truth.

4. **Empowerment**: The Holy Spirit empowers believers to live a Spirit-led life, naturally displaying the Fruit of the Spirit, such as love, joy, peace, patience, kindness, and self-control.

5. **Preparation for Faith Application**: The Holy Spirit prepares individuals to receive the objects of their faith by helping them gain the necessary knowledge and understanding and develop the necessary qualities, attitudes, and behaviors. Knowledge that is part of the preparation to receive objects of their request by faith.

6. **Personal Relationship with God**: The Holy Spirit facilitates communion with God, coordinating with the Spirit of God indwelling individuals and allowing them to experience His presence and guidance in their lives. To align their actions with the Will of God the Father.

In summary, the Holy Spirit is a divine helper that strengthens faith, reveals truth, and supports believers in their spiritual journey, enabling them to live a life aligned with God's will and purpose.

What is the Role of The Spirit of Truth in Faith?

According to the book, the **Spirit of Truth** plays a pivotal role in faith by helping individuals discern truth, providing confirmation of spiritual realities, and enhancing their ability to live a Spirit-led life. Here are the key roles of the Spirit of Truth in faith:

1. **Discernment of Truth**: The Spirit of Truth confirms truths revealed to individuals, ensuring that they are aligned with God's will. It helps believers recognize and accept spiritual realities, separating truth from error and fallacies.

2. **Purification of the Heart**: The Spirit of Truth purifies the human heart, leading individuals to formulate a life purpose based on the love of truth. It inspires believers to seek truth and live by it.

3. **Confirmation of Faith**: The Spirit of Truth provides assurance and confidence in the application of faith. It confirms that the actions taken by believers are in alignment with God's Will, strengthening their trust in Him.

4. **Motivation for Spiritual Growth**: The Spirit of Truth motivates individuals to progress spiritually, encouraging

them to seek truth, beauty, and goodness. It inspires believers to live a life of righteousness and service to others.

5. **Personal Revelation**: The Spirit of Truth works alongside the Spirit of God within individuals (called Thought Adjusters), revealing spiritual truths and guiding them in their journey of faith. It helps believers experience personal spiritual growth and enlightenment.

6. **Liberation**: The Spirit of Truth sets individuals free from the bondage of fear, guilt, and doubt, enabling them to live a life of spiritual liberty and confidence in their relationship with God.

In summary, the Spirit of Truth is a divine presence that enhances faith by confirming truth, purifying the heart, and providing assurance and guidance. It empowers believers to live a life of spiritual growth, service, and alignment with God's Will.

Why Asking for Help is Important in Faith

According to the book, **asking for help is a crucial aspect of faith** because it demonstrates humility, trust, and reliance on God as the ultimate source of provision and guidance. Here's why asking for help is important in faith:

1. **Acknowledging Dependence on God**: Asking for help is an act of humility that recognizes God as the Universal Father and the First Source and Center of all things. It shows that we trust Him to provide for our needs and desires.

2. **Activating Faith**: Asking is a key step in the process of applying faith. It sets the foundation for hope, belief, and trust, which are essential components of faith. By asking, we direct our faith toward a specific object or outcome.

3. **Obedience to God's Will**: The book, "The Five Keys To Prosperity" emphasizes that God desires His children to ask for what they need or desire. This act of asking aligns with His Will and opens the door for blessings and guidance.

4. **Overcoming Pride**: Asking for help requires setting aside pride and embracing humility. It allows us to acknowledge our limitations and seek divine intervention, which is essential for spiritual growth.

5. **Strengthening the Relationship with God**: When we ask for help, we deepen our personal relationship with God the Father, inviting Him into our lives and allowing Him to work through us in His own manner and time.

6. **Receiving Guidance**: Asking for help opens the way for God, the Holy Spirit, and ministering spirits to guide us toward the actions and opportunities necessary to manifest the objects of our faith.

In summary, asking for help is a key step in the faith process, as it reflects humility, trust, and a willingness to rely on God's guidance and provision. It is an essential act of faith that strengthens our spiritual connection and allows us to receive the blessings and support we need.

What "Substance" mean in this context of Faith

In the context of the book, 'substance' refers to the **real and essential element of faith** that gives it direction and purpose. It is the foundation upon which faith operates and manifests the desired outcomes. Here's a breakdown of its meaning:

1. **Essence of Faith**: Substance is described as the "real part or element of anything; the unchanging essence of something, reality." In faith, it represents the tangible or intangible object that is hoped for.

2. **The Object of Faith**: Substance is the thing you hope for, whether it is material, physical, or spiritual. It can be something you can perceive with your senses (e.g., a house, healing, or food) or something intangible (e.g., wisdom, understanding, or love).

3. **Foundation for Hope**: Substance provides faith with direction and purpose. It is the basis for hope, which fuels the belief and trust necessary for faith to work effectively.

4. **Spiritual and Material Reality**: Substance exists in both the spiritual and material realms. Even if the object of faith is not yet visible or tangible, it exists as a potential reality in the spiritual realm, waiting to be made manifest.

5. **True Meaning**: Substance also refers to the true content or meaning of a statement or belief. It is the truth that underpins faith and makes it effective.

In summary, **substance is the essence of the object of faith**—the thing hoped for—that provides faith with direction, purpose, and meaning. It bridges the gap between the spiritual and material realms, enabling the manifestation of faith to eventually come into the material, physical realm.

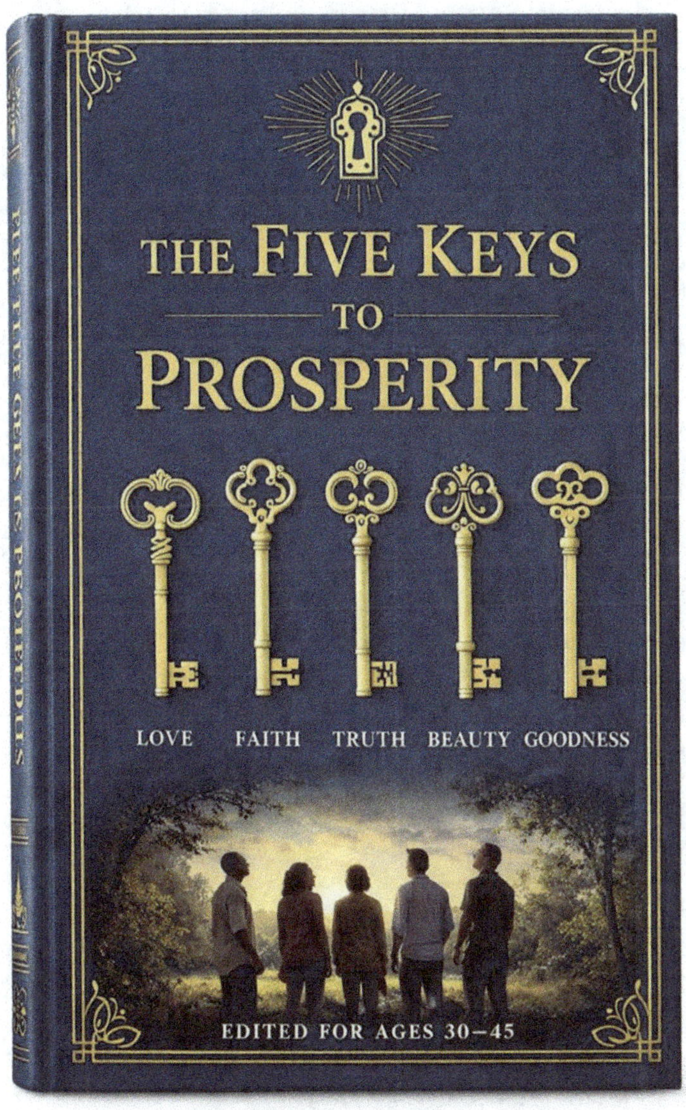
THE FIVE KEYS
TO
PROSPERITY
LOVE   FAITH   TRUTH   BEAUTY   GOODNESS
EDITED FOR AGES 30—45

www.ingramcontent.com/pod-product-compliance
Lightning Source LLC
Chambersburg PA
CBHW070317160726
47999CB00003B/1057